Secretarial Practice

:: Author ::

Hetal Parmar

(M.COM., M.phil., SLET)

PUBLISHED BY

Hemchadracharya International Publishing House
HQ. At & Po. Chaveli., Ta- Chansma,
Dist- Patan, North Gujarat, India, Asia.
www.iphouseindia.com

First Publication: 27TH January, 2015

Copyright: Author

(c) Hetal Parmar

ISBN:- 978-15-08712-17-6

Price: Rs.750/- INDIA
$ 15 OUTSIDE INDIA

PUBLISHED BY

Hemchadracharya International Publishing House
HQ. At & Po. Chaveli., Ta- Chansma,
Dist- Patan, North Gujarat, India, Asia.
www.iphouseindia.com

Content

Sr.no	Particulars	Page no.
Unit 01	**Company Secretary**	01
Unit 02	**Company and Types of Company**	35

Unit 01

COMPANY SECRETARY

1.0 Meaning of secretary & Company secretary

The word "Secretary" is derived from the Latin word **"Secretarius"** meaning Confidential Officer. A secretary is defined by the Oxford Dictionary as "one whose office is to write for another, especially one who is employed to conduct correspondence, to keep records and to transact various other businesses for another person or for a society, corporation or public body".

The Companies Act 1956, as amended by the Amendment Act of 1988, defines a secretary as "any individual possessing the prescribed qualifications appointed to perform the duties which may be performed by a Secretary under the Act and any other ministerial and administrative duties".

Therefore the Secretary is one of the principal officers of the company with the requisite qualifications to undertake secretarial work and management of the affairs of the company as per the provisions of the Act and instructions laid down by the Board of Directors. The Board, however, cannot alter the duties of the secretary as they are determined by the law.

1.1 TYPES OF SE-CRETARIES

There are various types of secretaries, such as 'private secretary, secretary to a club, cooperative society, government company, etc., A brief description of these types is as follows:

❖ PRIVATE SECRETARY

A private secretary is usually appointed by an important person such as a minister in the government, member of parliament, manager, business magnate or professional men like doctors, lawyers, etc, ' His work is to attend to the correspondence and other personal work or office work of the employer. Sometimes, the private secretary may also be entrusted with certain duties of a private nature such as handling banking transaction, arranging meeting, parties, and drafting reports and speeches.

❖ SECRETARY OF A CLUB OR ASSOCIATION

Non-profit making associations like Charitable institutions, cultural associations and professional association, sports and athletic clubs may appoint a full-time secretary to conduct the day-to-day activities of the association or club. As an honorary secretary cannot generally be expected to devote his entire time to the work of the association or the club, paid secretaries are appointed.

The important functions of the secretary of an association are:

1. The attend to administrative functions such as correspondence, maintenance of accounts and records, supervision of staff and arranging for the audit of the accounts.

2. To conduct activities of the club or association such as registration of new members, collection of fees, etc.

3. To convene meetings of members or executive committees and to prepare the required documents and minutes of the meetings.

4. To advise the managing committee on various matters relating to the association and to execute the decisions of the managing committee

❖ SECRETARY OF A CO-OPERATIVE SOCIETY

Generally, full-time secretaries are appointed in cooperative society. In some cases, one of the members of the managing committee may be elected to act as secretary.

The functions of the secretary of a cooperative society are:

1. To assist the managing committee in managing the affairs of the society.

2. To execute the decisions taken by the managing committee.

3. To maintain proper records and registers.

4. To arrange meetings and to attend conferences on behalf of the society.

❖ **SECRETARY OF A GOVERNMENT DEPARTMENT**

Each department of the government is under the control of a secretary, e.g., Secretary, Finance Department and Secretary, Education Department. He is also executive head and adviser to the minister who is concerned with that particular department.

The duties of a government secretary are:

1. Administrative and executive functions such as overall control and day-to-day administration of the office, guiding the subordinate officers of the department, coordinating the various activities of the department as well as the activities of allied department. Advisory functions, which include advising the minister on all matters regarding decisions and supplying whatever information is needed by the minister.

❖ SECRETARY OF A LOCAL BODY

Usually, municipal corporations and Panchayats appoint a paid secretary who will functions as an office executive. He is a link between the authorities and the staff. His functions are many and varied. He has to supervise and coordinate all activities of the office, prepare budgets, statements, arranging meetings, draft minutes, etc.,

❖ SECRETARY OF A TRADE UNION

Generally, every trade union appoints a secretary .He is a powerful person wielding much influence over the organized labourers. He is required to hold meeting of the union, to record their proceedings, to maintain accounts and statutory books and to conduct the correspondence on behalf of the union. He advises the 'union on various matters connected with labour .In case of disputes, he negotiates with the employers on behalf of the labour and makes efforts to settle the disputes.

❖ COMPANY SECRETARY

The secretary of a company guides the management in the day-to-day work of Company Law and mercantile law and of accounts, taxation, holding of meetings, drafting of reports. Resolutions etc. His duties are of ministerial and administrative character and he is not concerned with the directions. control or management of the affairs of the company. He is an officer of the company and his duties are multifarious but primarily they consist of duties to the Board, duties to the shareholders and duties to the company. Because of the vast expansion of joint stock forms of organisation, the position of secretary has become pre-eminent in the industrial and commercial world and has secured esteemed position and a high social status.

Section 2(45) of the companies Act of 1956, " A company secretary is a person who is a member of the Institute of the Company Secretaries of India or any other individual possessing the prescribed qualifications, appointed to perform the duties imposed on him by the companies Act, the ministerial or administrative duties and managerial functions that are delegated to him by the Board"

The Companies [Amendment] Act 19S5-provides that a company can appoint a secretary with 'limited executive' power of management delegated by the Board of Directors in addition to his routine duties. If the, Board entrusts the Secretary with routine duties, he is called, -'Routine Secretary', and if he is entrusted with limited executive managerial powers, he is called 'Executive Secretary'.

❖ ROUTINE SECRETARY

A Secretary is called a Routine Secretary because his position can be compared to the position of the head of a clerical department doing only such work as he is directed to do by the board. A routine secretary is just the mouth-piece of the Board of Directors. He has to do only what he is directed to do by the directors. He does not have any .

[7]

discretion of his own, and so, cannot do anything on his own. The duties of a routine secretary relate to:

1. To supervise issues of shares and debentures.

2. Registration of transfer and transmission of shares

3. Attending to work relating to board meetings and general meetings.

4. Preparing dividend warrants and maintaining the statutory and other books of the company.

5. Filing the necessary return of the company with the Registrar of the companies

❖ EXECUTIVE SECRETARY

When a secretary of a company, in addition to the performance of the routine office work, also acts as the Chief Executive Officer of the company, he becomes an executive secretary .In this case, he exercises managerial and administrative powers and performs many executive and managerial functions delegated to him by the board. So, he is called an Executive secretary.

An executive secretary, besides performing tile routine office work of a secretary, also performs a number of other responsible jobs. The other important duties of an executive secretary are:

1. To Organise and Control the whole office.

2. To carry on the correspondence work relating to the various departments of the Company.

3. To attend to all matters relating to the Cost and company accounts.

4. To negotiate contracts with third parties on behalf of the Company.

5. To act as a Liaison officer, i.e., Establishing links between the company and outsiders.

6. To act as an adviser and guide to the board of directors on all important matters of policy and administration.

1.2 APPOINTMENT OF A COMPANY SECRETARY

As per the Indian Companies Act, 1956, it was not compulsory for companies to appoint a secretary. However, in practice all companies appointed secretaries. As per Rule 2(1) of Companies [Appointment and Qualification of Secretary (Amendment)] Rules. 1993 it is obligatory for a company having a paid-up capital of not less than Rs. 50

Lakhs to appoint a whole-time secretary. As per Rule 2(1) above for companies having paid-up capital of less than Rs. 50 lakhs it is not obligatory to appoint a whole-time secretary .Further, when the board of directors of any such company comprises only two directors, neither of them shall be secretary of the company. The Act also states that no individual can hold the office 'of 'secretary in more than one such company. Further, only a individual possessing such qualifications as the central Government may prescribe can be appointed as secretary of a company. Now, a company having paid-up capital of Rs. 2 crores must have a whole time secretary. [This came into force from 11th June 2002].

The promoters of the company generally first appointment a secretary who assists them in he formation of the company by attending to all preliminary work such as preparation of various documents and statements required for registering the company, arranging the meetings of the promoters, preparation of minutes, etc,. He is often referred to as **Protem Secretary** (i.e. secretary for the time being) and his name may be included in the Articles of Association of the Company. If the board of directors decides to appoint another person as secretary other then the **Protem Secretary** after incorporation of the company, the first secretary who is appointment by the promoters cannot sue the company. However, he should be given proper notice in such a case, otherwise, he can sue the company for damages. Hence, to secure his position, the first secretary who has been acting, as *Protem Secretary* must, immediately after the incorporation, get his appointment confirmed by a resolution at the first board meeting.

The procedure for appointing a company secretary. other than the first secretary .is as follows:

1. A resolution has be passed at the board of directors' meeting appointing a secretary on certain terms and conditions.

2. The particulars of appointment must be filed ill duplicate with the Registrar within 30 days of the appointment.

3. I the person appointed as secretary functions as secretary in any other company, he to notify the other company within 20 days of his appointment.

4. Any director interested in the appointment of secretary must disclose his intent and must not take part in the discussion or voting on the resolution.

5. If the person appointed, as secretary is the director of a company or is a relative of a director, a special resolution h-as to be passed in the general board meeting for such an appointment.

The following persons are usually not qualified for appointment as the secretary in a public limited company:

1. A director of a company

2. The auditor of the company

3. Any other person who is not eligible to enter into a contract.

The reasons for disqualifying the above persons are that the post of a secretary is deemed to be a post of profit and the companies Act 1956 stipulates that no director can hold any place of profit. But by obtaining the consent of a company by assigning a special resolution a director can be appointed as a secretary. It should, however, be noted that in case a director is appointed as a secretary, he cannot continue as a director.

As regards auditor as a secretary of a company, the Act states that no employee of a company can act as auditor. As such we find that a secretary is an employee of a company and therefore, a person cannot be appointed both as a secretary and as auditor of a company.

1.3 DUTIES AND FUNCTIONS OF COMPANY SECRETARY

The duties of .a secretary vary from company to company, depending upon the nature on the business, size of the company and the powers enjoyed by and responsibilities entrusted with the secretary.

The duties of a company secretary may be classified under the following broad heads:

1. Statutory duties

2. General Duties

    a. Duties in relation to directors

    b. Duties in relation to shareholders

    c. Duties towards organisation and office

    d. Duties in relation to the public

1. STATUTORY DUTIES

The statutory duties of a company secretary are those prescribed by the Companies Act or by any other legislation such as the Income Tax Act, Sales tax Act, Stamp Act, Employee state. Insurance Act, Industrial Disputes Acts, Contract Act, Monopolies and Restrictive Trade Practices Act, etc,

The most important part of his statutory duties relates to the various provisions of the Companies Act are:

1. Maintenance of books and registers of the company

2. Filing of the necessary returns with the Registrar of Companies

3. Supervising the issue, allotment, transfer and forfeiture of share and debentures.

4. Attending to meetings and recording their proceedings.

5. Safe Custody and proper use of the common seal of the company.

    ➢ The Income-tax Act requires him to take steps for the deduction of income tax from dividends, interest and salary and its payment to the tax authorities.

➢ Under the Stamp Act, he has to see that stamps of the requisite amount are affixed to documents, shares etc.,

➢ Under the Sales-tax Act, he has to arrange for timely submission of returns and payment of tax. In addition, he has to comply with the provisions of any other Act which is applicable to that particular company. For instance, a manufacturing company has to comply with the provisions of the Factories Act, the Industrial Disputes Act, Minimum Wages Act and other Industrial laws. The secretary has to see that these provisions are complied with.

➢ A company secretary is not only a servant of the company but also a servant of the law.

2. GENERAL DUTIES

➢ Duties in Relation to Directors:

The Secretary has to look after the correspondence with the director, convene board meetings under the direction, of the managing director, prepare minutes and execute the orders and instruction of the board. He has to advise the directors during the deliberations at the meeting regarding the provisions of various Acts. He acts as a guide to the board of directors.

The secretary is the confidential clerk of the board. While the directors lay down the broad policies of the company at board meetings, the secretary interprets these policies. He communicates board decisions to the staff and shareholders and because of this, he is called the mouthpiece of the board of directors. Further, the secretary has to keep the board posted with all developments relating to the activities of the company. As the secretary is the agent of the board of directors, he must carry out their instructions. In addition he keeps the common seal of the company and uses it as directed by the board.

> **Duties in Relation to Shareholders.**

The secretary is also medium of communication between the company and shareholders. -As the shareholders are the owners of the company, the secretary has to safeguard their interest and should attend to their enquires regarding payment of dividend, issues of share, etc., In dealing with shareholders the secretary has to be very tactful and, at the same time, be courteous, friendly and helpful. He has to ensure that no confidential information of the company is made available to a section of the members, which may affect the interest of the company as a whole. . Further, he has to organize and supervise correspondence with shareholders with regard to the following:

1. Application and allotment of shares.
2. Calls of shares.
3. Forfeiture of shares.
4. Transfer and transmission of shares.
5. Distribution of dividend
6. Notice and circulars to .members
7. Meetings of shareholders
8. Inquiries and complaints from shareholders.

➤ **Miscellaneous or other Duties:**

The other duties of a company secretary are:

1. He should not act without authority
2. He should discharge his duties honestly
3. He should Exercise reasonable care & diligence
4. He should Act in & emergency very cautiously in the interest of the company

5. He should not leak out the secrets or confidential matters

of the company either to the share holders or to the Public.

6. He should represent the company on social functions.

➢ **Duties towards Organization and Office.**

The secretary is generally recognized as the head of the office of the company and has control over departments such as shares, record and filing, accounts and statistics. He has to ensure that the office works with maximum efficiency. He has to supervise various activities of the office and also coordinate the activities of the different departments. In order to get the best out of the staff, he has the overall duty to select, organize and guide personnel. This requires that he should devote particular attention to the terms and conditions of their service and also maintain personal contact with individual members of the staff.

➢ **Duties in Relation to the Public.**

The secretary being in possession of all-important information about the various aspects of the company has to function as a medium of communication between the directors and the general public consisting of debenture holders, bankers, solicitors, creditors and the 'prospective investors. He has to be in touch with them and provide information that may be asked for. At the same time, he should take care to see that no confidential information is divulged to the public. Further, he should function as liaison officer between the shareholders and the directors, the company and the outsiders and should discharge his duties in the best interest of the company.

1.4 QUALIFICATIONS OF THE SECRETARY

In the case of companies with a paid-up share capital of less than Rs. 2 crores any individual possessing any go the following qualifications may be appointed as 'its whole-time secretary to perform of duties of secretary.

(I) Membership of the Institute of Company secretary of India (ICST).

(II) Pass in the intermediate examination conducted by the Institute of Company Secretary in India (ICSI).

(III) Post-Graduate degree in commerce or corporate secretaryship awarded by any university in India.

(IV) Degree in Law awarded by any university.

(V) Membership of the Institute of Cost and. Works Accountants of India.

(VI) Membership of the Institute of Chartered Accountants of India.

(VII) Post-graduate in Company Law and Secretarial Practice granted by the University of Udaipur.

(VIII) Membership of the Association of Secretaries and Manager, Calcutta.

(IX) Diploma in Corporate Laws and Management granted by the India Law Institute, New Delhi.

(X) Post-graduate degree or diploma in Management Sciences granted by any University.

(XI) Post-graduate degree or diploma granted by Indian Institutes of Management, Bangalore, Calcutta, Lucknow, Ahmedabad or Calicut.

The qualifications possessed by a person holding the office as the secretary of a company immediately before 30the October 1980 shall be deemed to be the qualification, which he shall he required to possess in order to be eligible to continue in that company.

The Company (Secretary qualification) Rules stated above, do not apply to a limited company which is formed for the promotion of commerce, arts and science, religion, charity etc,. and which makes priority payment of dividends to its members (i.e. a company to which a license is granted under Section 25 of the Companies Act).

1.5 QUALITIES OF THE COMPANY SECRETARY:

In addition to the statutory qualifications, a company secretary should possess certain other qualities if he is to discharge his multifarious duties efficiently. The qualities are:

> **Sound General Education:** A sound general education helps the secretary in grasping the subject without taking much of his time and effort.

> **Command over Languages:** As a large part of the secretary's work consists of correspondence and preparation of report and précis, it is necessary that he should have a command over language. Further, he should also be conversant with certain specialized business terms and expressions suited to his work. If his company has

foreign connections, it is better for him to have a knowledge of one or two foreign languages.

➢ **Knowledge of Office Administration:** For the efficient organisation of the office, the secretary should know the best system of filing and indexing and should have a knowledge of labour saving devices, recruitment of office staff, methods of remuneration, delegation of work etc.,

➢ **Knowledge of Accounting and Taxation:** As company secretary is an executive office of the company, he must also have a basic knowledge of the principles of accounting and taxation, consisting of income tax and sales tax.

➢ **Knowledge of Company Law:** A thorough knowledge of the various provisions of the Companies, Act is essential for the secretary .Companies have to function within the legal framework of the companies Act, hence a thorough knowledge of .the various provisions of Companies Act is essential for a secretary.

➢ **Knowledge of various acts Relating to Staff:** For the efficient handling of staff, the secretary should have thorough knowledge of various acts of legislation which are applicable to the staff, viz., the Factories Act, the Industrial Disputes Act, the Workmen's Compensation Act, the Employees' Provident Fund Act, the Payment of Wages Act, Income Tax Act, etc.

➢ **Knowledge of Mercantile Law:** Apart from the knowledge of the law relating to staff, a working knowledge of the laws relating to contracts, negotiable instruments, sale of goods, insurance etc, may be of immense help to the secretary in discharging his duties.

➢ **Knowledge of the Industry:** He should have a thorough knowledge of the business of his company and knowledge of the industry in which his company is engaged. This would help him to give proper guidance to the chairmen and the board on various intricacies of business.

➢ **General Knowledge:** General Knowledge helps the secretary in guiding the chairman and board of directors, and in performing his duties confidently. Hence, apart from knowledge of the industry, the secretary should have general knowledge likes current happenings, economic conditions, political and social condition, market conditions, etc.

Impressive personality:

The various qualifications and qualities mentioned above are essential, but not sufficient. Besides these, for a company secretary to be successful executive, he must have a good personality which is a comprehensive term consisting of so many personal virtues and talents such as charming manners, organizing ability, imagination, initiative, strong common sense, originality, efficiency arid intelligence, a sense of responsibility, alertness, self-discipline, foresight, industriousness, courtesy and high moral character .

Rights

The rights of a company secretary mostly flow out of his service agreement with the company. These may be summarized as follows:

1. Right to supervise the secretarial department. Being head of the secretarial department, he has the right to control and supervise the activities of the department under his control

2. Right to sign documents. As a principal officer within the meaning of the Companies Act, he has to sign documents requiring authentication of the company

3. Right to claim remuneration. The secretary is a servant (employee) of the company and has a right to claim his salary during its lifetime. Before his services are terminated, he can demand a reasonable notice and claim damages for his wrongful dismissal. In the event of the winding up of the company he can claim his outstanding salary as a preferential creditor

But the secretary has no right to:

1. Make allotment, or register transfer, of shares of the company unless he is specifically authorised by the directors in that behalf and the Articles of the company allow the directors to delegate this power to the secretary

2. Make any representation on behalf of the company or to enter into any contracts without express authority and consent of the directors;

3. Borrow in the name of the company

1.6 LIABILITIES OF THE SECRETARY

The liabilities of the company secretary may be divided into two categories:

a) Statutory liabilities

b) Contractual liabilities

a) Statutory Liabilities

As the principal executive officer of the company, the secretary has certain statutory obligations under the Companies Act, Income tax Act and the Stamp Act, Sales tax Act etc. If the secretary fails to carry out the statutory obligations or duties imposed on him by the various acts, certain liabilities are imposed on him by the Companies Act and other acts. Such liabilities are called the Statutory liabilities. In short, statutory liabilities refer to all those liabilities imposed on the secretary by the Companies Act and other acts for his failure to discharge his statutory duties. The various statutory liabilities imposed on the company secretary are:

1. If he fails to hold a statutory meeting.

2. If he does not circulate the statutory report.

3. If he fails to hold the Annual General Meeting.

4. If he fails to submit to the Registrar of Companies copies of annual accounts and other statements.

5. If he fails to give notice of Board Meeting.

6. If he fails to record the minutes of Board and General Meeting.

7. If he does not maintain minute books at the registered office.

8. If he refuses to allow inspection of minutes by the members.

9. If he refuses to furnish copies of Minutes to members.

10. If he fails in making ready share certificates and debenture certificates within the stipulated period.

11. If he fails to maintain a register of directors, shareholders and debenture holders.

12. If he fails to comply with the provisions of the Act regarding the appointment of auditors and the auditor's report.

13. If he fails to rectify the mistake within a period of two months, in case the company has been registered by a name which is identical with or too closely resembles the name of an existing company.

14. If he fails in filing With the Registrar of the Companies relevant documents as required by the Act.

15. If he fails in registering the resolutions etc, as required.

16. If he fails to have the name of the company engraved on the seals, etc.

17. If he fails to make entries in the member's register on the issue of share warrants.

18. If he fails to comply with the provisions of this Act particularly regarding the appointment of auditor, audit reports, etc.

19. Under the Income Tax Act, 1961 the company secretary is responsible for collection and payment of income tax.

20. Under the Indian Stamp Act, the company secretary is responsible for verifying the correctness of documents needing stamps, etc.

b) Contractual Liabilities

Apart from the statutory liabilities, the company secretary has certain liabilities to the company arising out of his contract of service with the company. These liabilities are known as contractual liabilities.

1. He must carry out the orders given to him by the directors.

2. He must carry out the obligations of his service Agreement with the company.

3. He should not disclose any confidential information of The company.

4. He should not do anything beyond his authority. If he Acts beyond his authority, he will be held personally liable for any damage or loss suffered by the company or any third party as a result of his action.

5. He is expected to perform his duties .with reasonable Care and skill.

6. He is liable for damages caused to the company by his wilful misconduct and neglect of duties.

7. He is liable for any fraud on the part of any of hi assistants if it is proved that he is a pally to such fraud.

1.7 LEGAL POSITION OF THE SECRETARY

The Companies Act has recognised the secretary as the principal officer of the company and he is responsible for the secretarial and other purely ministerial and administrative work of the company. He has to file various returns and statements with the Registrar of Companies as per the requirements of the Companies Act. In case he fails to fulfil these statutory obligations, he will be held liable for such defaults.

In the eyes of law, **the secretary is a mere servant of the company.** He has to act in accordance with the order or directions of the board of directors. Without authority, he cannot enter into any contract with the third parties and cannot make any representation on behalf of the company. He is appointed by the board and derives his authority from the board. He is under the control of the board of directors and he has to carry out the orders of the board and cannot exercise independent discretion in the work for which he is responsible. Thus, the secretary is a mere servant and subordinate officer of the company without any managerial function.

ACTUAL POSITION OR STATUS OF A COMPANY SECRET

The actual position of a company secretary is not merely that of a servant or an agent, but something more than that. In actual practice, a company secretary occupies a position of importance in the administrative set-up of the company. He is not a mere tool in tlle hands of the board of directors or the mouth piece of the directors carrying out the orders of the directors. In the company set up, both the board of directors and the: secretary play .a complementary role to each other. The board of directors is responsible for the overall management of the company's business. It plans, decides and formulates the policies of the company. But the responsibility of the actual execution of the policies lies with the company secretary .It is the secretary who carries out the orders of the board of directors. That is why, it has been rightly remarked that while the directors are the brain of the company, the secretary is its eyes, ears and hands of the company.

The company secretary is in close touch with the work of the board and has access to the confidential matters of the company. He exercises his discretion in most matters relating to the routine affairs of the company. Similarly, in matters relating to staff, shareholders and. outsiders, generally, the secretary is allowed .to exercise his discretionary power. This power of discretion is given to the board because the directors may not be in a position to devote their time for taking decisions relating to matters which are of a routine nature. He is often consulted by the chairman and the board before taking any decision on policy matters or on any other important matter since he, has an intimate knowledge of the company and is in constant touch with the staff, the shareholders and the public. He is in a better position to advise the board on various matters relating to the functioning of the company. Further, as he possess a thorough knowledge of the various legislative enactments relating to companies, he is consulted by the board on various legal matters.

The company secretary acts in different capacities and discharges many duties and responsibilities. They are:

1. He acts as the agent of the board of directors and carries out the instructions of the board of directors.

2. He acts as the registrar of the company and attends to the secretarial functions, such as the filing of various returns and statements with the registrar of companies, registration of transfers and transmission of shares and the work of correspondence.

3. He serves as the business executive of the company and carries out the routine office work and also the managerial duties entrusted to him by the board.

4. He acts as an adviser and advises the directors and the chairman on important matters affecting the business of the company.

5. He acts as a liaison officer between the board of directors on the one side and the staff, shareholders and the general public on the other side.

6. He acts as a confidential officer and ensures that the confidential matters of the company are not leaked out.

7. He is also required to act as a public relations officer of the company and improve the image of the company in the minds of the public.

1.8 REMOVAL OR DISMISSAL OF A COMPANY SECRETARY

The Secretary may be removed from office by the board of directors, under the power expressly given in the articles or under their general powers which the articles generally give them. A secretary being a servant of the company, his suspension and dismissal are governed by the normal law applicable to employer and employee. The services of a secretary may be terminated by giving him notice as per the terms of the service agreement. If an agreement does not mention any specific period of notice, reasonable notice must be given.

The services of the secretary may be terminated without notice if he makes profits secretly. He may be dismissed for willful disobedience, misconduct, negligence, fraud; dishonesty, and permanent disability .The appointment of a receiver or manager in a debenture holder's action (suit) against the company, or making of an order by the court for compulsory winding up of the company will operate as a termination of the services of the secretary.

Unit 02

Company and types of company

2.0 OBJECTIVE

After reading this lesson, you should be able to:

(a) Define a company and explain its features.

(b) Make a distribution between company and partnership firm.

(c) Explain the various types of companies.

2.1 INTRODUCTION

Industrial has revolution led to the emergence of large scale business organizations. These organization require big investments and the risk involved is very high. Limited resources and unlimited liability of partners are two important limitations of partnerships of partnerships in undertaking big business. Joint Stock Company form of business organization has become extremely popular as it provides a solution to overcome the limitations of partnership business. The Multinational companies like Coca-Cola and, General Motors have their investors and customers spread throughout the world. The giant Indian Companies may include the names like Reliance, Talco Bajaj

Auto, Infosys Technologies, Hindustan Lever Ltd., Ranbaxy Laboratories Ltd., and Larsen and Turbo etc.

2.2 MEANING OF COMPANY

Section 3 (1) (i) of the Companies Act, 1956 defines a company as "a company formed and registered under this Act or an existing company". Section 3(1) (ii) Of the act states that "an existing company means a company formed and registered under any of the previous companies laws". This definition does not reveal the distinctive characteristics of a company . According to Chief Justice Marshall of USA, "A company is a person, artificial, invisible, intangible, and existing only in the contemplation of the law. Being a mere creature of law, it possesses only those properties which the character of its creation of its creation confers upon it either expressly or as incidental to its very existence".

Another comprehensive and clear definition of a company is given by Lord Justice Lindley, "A company is meant an association of many persons who contribute money or money's worth to a common stock and employ it in some trade or business, and who share the profit and loss (as the case may be) arising there from. The common stock contributed is denoted in money and is the capital of the company. The persons who contribute it, or to whom it belongs, are members. The proportion of capital to which each member is entitled is his share. Shares are always transferable although the right to transfer them is often more or less restricted". According to Haney, "Joint Stock Company is a voluntary association of individuals for profit, having a capital divided into transferable shares. The ownership of which is the condition of membership".

From the above definitions, it can be concluded that a company is registered association which is an artificial legal person, having an independent legal, entity with a perpetual succession, a common seal for its signatures, a common capital comprised of transferable shares and carrying limited liability.

2.3 CHARACTERISTICS OF A COMPANY

The main characteristics of a company are :

1. Incorporated association. A company is created when it is registered under the Companies Act. It comes into being from the date mentioned in the certificate of incorporation. It

[37]

may be noted in this connection that Section 11 provides that an association of more than ten persons carrying on business in banking or an association or more than twenty persons carrying on any other type of business must be registered under the Companies Act and is deemed to be an illegal association, if it is not so registered.

For forming a public company at least seven persons and for a private company at least two persons are persons are required. These persons will subscribe their names to the Memorandum of association and also comply with other legal requirements of the Act in respect of registration to form and incorporate a company, with or without limited liability   [Sec 12 (1)]

2.   **Artificial legal person.** A company is an artificial person. Negatively speaking, it is not a natural person. It exists in the eyes of the law and cannot act on its own. It has to act through a board of directors elected by shareholders. It was rightly pointed out in Bates V Standard Land Co. that : "The board of directors are the brains and the only brains of the company, which is the body and the company can and

does act only through them".

But for many purposes, a company is a legal person like a natural person. It has the right to acquire and dispose of the property, to enter into contract with third parties in its own name, and can sue and be sued in its own name.

However, it is not a citizen as it cannot enjoy the rights under the Constitution of India or Citizenship Act. In State Trading Corporation of India v C.T.O (1963 SCJ 705), it was held that neither the provisions of the Constitution nor the Citizenship Act apply to it. It should be noted that though a company does not possess fundamental rights, yet it is person in the eyes of law. It can enter into contracts with its Directors, its members, and outsiders.

Justice Hidayatullah once remarked that if all the members are citizens of India, the company does not become a citizen of India.

3. **Separate Legal Entity :** A company has a legal distinct entity and is independent of its members. The creditors of the company can recover their money only from the company and the property of the company. They cannot sue individual members. Similarly, the company is not in any way liable for

the individual debts of its members. The property of the company is to be used for the benefit of the company and nor for the personal benefit of the shareholders. On the same grounds, a member cannot claim any ownership rights in the assets of the company either individually or jointly during the existence of the company or in its winding up. At the same time the members of the company can enter into contracts with the company in the same manner as any other individual can. Separate legal entity of the company is also recognized by the Income Tax Act. Where a company is required to pay Income-tax on its profits and when these profits are distributed to shareholders in the form of dividend, the shareholders have to pay income-tax on their dividend of income. This proves that a company that a company and its shareholders are two separate entities.

The principal of separate of legal entity was explained and emphasized in the famous case of Salomon v Salomon & Co. Ltd.

The facts of the case are as follows :

Mr. Saloman, the owner of a very prosperous shoe

business, sold his business for the sum of Rs. 39,000 to Saloman and Co. Ltd. which consisted of Saloman himself, his wife, his daughter and his four sons. The purchase consideration was paid by the company by allotment of & 20,000 shares and Rs. 10,000 debentures and the balance in cash to Mr. Saloman. The debentures carried a floating charge on the assets of the company. One share of Rs. 1 each was subscribed by the remaining six members of his family. Saloman and his two sons became the directors of this company. Saloman was the managing Director.

After a short duration, the company went into liquidation. At that time the statement of affairs' was like this: Assets :   Rs.6000, liabilities; Salomanas debenture holder Rs. 10,000 and unsecured creditors Rs. 7,000. Thus its assets were running short of its liabilities b Rs.11,000

The unsecured creditors claimed a priority over the debenture holder on the ground that company and Saloman were one and the same person. But the House of Lords held that the existence of a company is quite independent and distinct from its members and that the assets of the company must be utilized in payment of the debentures first in priority to unsecured creditors.

Saloman's case established beyond doubt that in law a registered company is an entity distinct from its members, even if the person hold all the shares in the company. There is no difference in principle between a company consisting of only two shareholders and a company consisting of two hundred members. In each case the company is a separate legal entity.

The principle established in Saloman's case also been applied in the following: Lee V. Lee's Airforming Ltd. (1961) A.C. 12 Of the 3000 shares in Lee's Air Forming Ltd., Lee held 2999 shares. He voted himself the managing Director and also became Chief Pilot of the company on a salary. He died in an aircrash while working for the company. His wife was granted compensation for the husband in the course of employment. Court held that Lee was a separate person from the company he formed, and compensation was due to the widow. Thus, the rule of corporate personality enabled

Lee to be the master and servant at the same time.

The principle of separate legal entity of a company has been, in fact recognized much earlier than in Saloman's case. In Re Kondoi Tea Co Ltd. (1886 ILR 13 Cal 43), it was held by Calcutta High Court that a company was a separate person, a separate body altogether from its Shareholders. In Re. Sheffield etc. Society - 22 OBD 470), it has been held that a corporation is a legal person, just as much in individual but with no physical existence.

The characteristic of separate corporate personality of a company was also emphasized by Chief Justice Marshall of USA when he defined a company "as a person, artificial, invisible, intangible and existing only in the eyes of the law. Being a mere creation of law, it possesses only those properties which the charter of its creation confers upon it either expressly or as accident to its very existence". [Trustees of Darmouth College v woodward (1819) 17 US 518)

4. Perpetual Existence. A company is a stable form of business organization. Its life does not depend upon the death, insolvency or retirement of any or all shareholder (s) or director (s). Law creates it and law alone can dissolve it.

Members may come and go but the company can go on forever. "During the war all the member of one private company, while in general meeting, were killed by a bomb. But the company survived; not even a hydrogen bomb could have destroyed". The company may be compared with a flowing river where the water keeps on changing continuously, still the identity of the river remains the same. Thus, a company has a perpetual existence, irrespective of changes in its membership.

5.   **Common Seal.** As was pointed out earlier, a company being an artificial person has no body similar to natural person and as such it cannot sign documents for itself. It acts through natural person who are called its directors. But having a legal personality, it can be bound by only those documents which bear its signature. Therefore, the law has provided for the use of common seal, with the name of the company engraved on it, as a substitute for its signature. Any document bearing the common seal of the company will be legally binding on the company. A company may have its own regulations in its Articles of Association for the manner

of affixing the common seal to a document. If the Articles are silent, the provisions of Table-A (the model set of articles appended to the Companies Act) will apply. As per regulation 84 of Table-A the seal of the company shall not be affixed to any instrument except by the authority of a resolution of the Board or a Committee of the Board authorized by it in that behalf, and except in the presence of at least two directors and of the secretary or such other person as the Board may appoint for the purpose, and those two directors and the secretary or other person aforesaid shall sign every instrument to which the seal of the company is so affixed in their presence.

6.   Limited Liability : A company may be company limited by shares or a company limited by guarantee. In company limited by shares, the liability of members is limited to the unpaid value of the shares. For example, if the face value of a share in a company is Rs. 10 and a member has already paid Rs. 7 per share, he can be called upon to pay not more than Rs. 3 per share during the lifetime of the company. In a company limited by guarantee the liability of members is limited to such amount as the member may undertake to contribute to the assets of the company in the event of its being wound up.

7.   Transferable Shares. In a public company, the shares are freely transferable. The right to transfer shares is a statutory right and it cannot be taken away by a provision in the articles. However, the articles shall prescribe the manner in which such transfer of shares will be made and it may also contain bona fide and reasonable restrictions on the right of members to transfer their shares. But absolute restrictions on the rights of members to transfer their shares shall be ultra virus. However, in the case of a private company, the articles shall restrict the right of member to transfer their shares in companies with its statutory definition.

In order to make the right to transfer shares more effective, the shareholder can apply to the Central Government in case of refusal by the company to register a transfer of shares.

8. Separate Property : As a company is a legal person distinct from its members, it is capable of owning, enjoying and disposing of property in its own name. Although its capital and assets are contributed by its shareholders, they are not the private and joint owners of its property. The company is the real person in which all its property is vested and by which it is controlled, managed and disposed of.

9. Delegated Management : A joint stock company is an

autonomous, self-governing and self-controlling organization. Since it has a large number of members, all of them cannot take part in the management of the affairs of the company. Actual control and management is, therefore, delegated by the shareholders to their elected representatives, know as directors. They look after the day-to-day working of the company. Moreover, since shareholders, by majority of votes, decide the general policy of the company, the management of the company is carried on democratic lines. Majority decision and centralized management compulsorily bring about unity of action. **2.5 TYPES OF COMPANY**

Joint stock company can be of various types. The following are the important types of company:

1. **Classification of Companies by Mode of Incorporation**

   Depending on the mode of incorporation, there are three classes of joint stock companies.

A. **Chartered companies.** These are incorporated under a special charter by a monarch. The East India Company and The Bank of England are examples of chartered incorporated in England. The powers and nature of business of a chartered company are defined by the charter which incorporates it. A chartered company has wide powers. It can deal with its property and bind itself to any contracts that any ordinary person can. In case the company deviates from its business as prescribed by the charted, the Sovereign can annul the latter and close the company. Such companies do not exist in India.

B. **Statutory Companies.** These companies are incorporated by a Special Act passed by the Central or State legislature. Reserve Bank of India, State Bank of India, Industrial Finance Corporation, Unit Trust of India, State Trading corporation and Life Insurance Corporation are some of the examples of statutory companies. Such companies do not have any memorandum or articles of association. They derive their powers from the Acts constituting them and enjoy certain powers that companies incorporated under the Companies Act have. Alternations in the powers of such companies can be brought about by legislative amendments.

The provisions of the Companies Act shall apply to these companies also except in so far as provisions of the Act are inconsistent with those of such Special Acts [Sec 616 (d)]

These companies are generally formed to meet social needs and not for the purpose of earning profits.

C. Registered or incorporated companies. These are formed under the Companies Act, 1956 or under the Companies Act passed earlier to this. Such companies come into existence only when they are registered under the Act and a certificate of incorporation has been issued by the Registrar of Companies. This is the most popular mode of incorporating a company. Registered companies may further be divided into three categories of the following.

i) Companies limited by Shares : These types of companies have a share capital and the liability of each member or the company is limited by the Memorandum to the extent of face value of share subscribed by him. In other words, during the existence of the company or in the event of winding up, a member can be called upon to pay the amount remaining unpaid on the shares subscribed by him. Such a company is called company limited by shares. A company limited by shares may be a public company or a private company. These are the most popular types of companies.

ii) **Companies Limited by Guarantee :** These types of companies may or may not have a share capital. Each member promises to pay a fixed sum of money specified in the Memorandum in the event of liquidation of the company for payment of the debts and liabilities of the company [Sec 13(3)] This amount promised by him is called 'Guarantee'. The Articles of Association of the company state the number of member with which the company is to be registered [Sec 27 (2)]. Such a company is called a company limited by guarantee. Such companies depend for their existence on entrance and subscription fees. They may or may not have a share capital. The liability of the member is limited to the extent of the guarantee and the face value of the shares subscribed by them, if the company has a share capital. If it has a share capital, it may be a public company or a private company.

The amount of guarantee of each member is in the nature of reserve capital. This amount cannot be called upon except in the event of winding up of a company. Non-

trading or non-profit companies formed to promote culture, art, science, religion, commerce, charity, sports etc. are generally formed as companies limited by guarantee. **iii) Unlimited Companies :** Section 12 gives choice to the promoters to form a company with or without limited liability. A company not having any limit on the liability of its members is called an 'unlimited company' [Sec 12(c)]. An unlimited company may or may not have a share capital. If it has a share capital it may be a public company or a private company. If the company has a share capital, the article shall state the amount of share capital with which the company is to be registered [Sec 27 (1)]

The articles of an unlimited company shall state the number of member with which the company is to be registered.

II. On the Basis of Number of Members

On the basis of number of members, a company may be :

(1) Private Company, and (2) Public Company.

A. Private Company

According to Sec. 3(1) (iii) of the Indian Companies Act, 1956, a private company is that company which by its articles of association :

i)   limits the number of its members to fifty, excluding employees who are members or ex-employees who were and continue to be members;

ii)   restricts the right of transfer of shares, if any;

iii)   prohibits any invitation to the public to subscribe for any shares or debentures of the company.

Where two or more persons hold share jointly, they are treated as a single member. According to Sec 12 of the Companies Act, the minimum number of members to form a private company is two. A private company must use the word "Pvt" after its name.

Characteristics or Features of a Private Company. The main features of a private of a private company are as follows :

i)   A private company restricts the right of transfer of its shares. The shares of a private company are not as freely transferable as those of public companies.

The articles generally state that whenever a shareholder of a Private Company wants to transfer his shares, he must first offer them to the existing members of the existing members of the company. The price of the shares is determined by the directors. It is done so as to preserve the family nature of the company's shareholders.

ii) It limits the number of its members to fifty excluding members who are employees or ex-employees who were and continue to be the member. Where two or more persons hold share jointly they are treated as a single member. The minimum number of members to form a private company is two.

iv) A private company cannot invite the public to subscribe

for its capital or shares of debentures. It has to make its

own private arrangement.

B. Public company

According to Section 3 (1) (iv) of Indian Companies Act. 1956 "A public company which is not a Private Company",

If we explain the definition of Indian Companies Act. 1956 in regard to the public company, we note the following :

i)   The articles do not restrict the transfer of shares of the company

ii)   It imposes no restriction no restriction on the maximum number of the members on the company.

iii) It invites the general public to purchase the shares and debentures of the companies

(Differences between a Public Company and a Private company)

1. **Minimum number :** The minimum number of persons required to form a public company is 7. It is 2 in case of a private company.

2. **Maximum number :** There is no restriction on maximum number of members in a public company, whereas the maximum number cannot exceed 50 in a private company.

[55]

3. **Number of directors.** A public company must have at least 3 directors whereas a private company must have at least 2 directors (Sec. 252)

4. **Restriction on appointment of directors.** In the case of a public company, the directors must file with the Register a consent to act as directors or sign an undertaking for their qualification shares. The directors or a private company need not do so (Sec 266)

5. **Restriction on invitation to subscribe for shares.** A public company invites the general public to subscribe for shares. A public company invites the general public to subscribe for the shares or the debentures of the company. A private company by its Articles prohibits invitation to public to subscribe for its shares.

6. **Name of the Company :** In a private company, the words "Private Limited" shall be added at the end of its name.

7. **Public subscription :** A private company cannot invite the public to purchase its shares or debentures. A public company may do so.

8. **Issue of prospectus :** Unlike a public company a private company is not expected to issue a prospectus or file a statement in lieu of prospectus with the Registrar before allotting shares.

9. **Transferability of Shares.** In a public company, the shares are freely transferable (Sec. 82). In a private company the right to transfer shares is restricted by Articles.

10. **Special Privileges.** A private company enjoys some special privileges. A public company enjoys no such privileges.

11. **Quorum.** If the Articles of a company do not provide for a larger quorum. 5 members personally present in the case of a public company are quorum for a company It is 2 in the case of a private company (Sec. 174).

12. **Managerial remuneration.** Total managerial remuneration in a public company cannot exceed 11 per cent of the net profits (Sec. 198). No such restriction applies to a private company.

13. **Commencement of business.** A private company may commence its business immediately after obtaining a

certificate of incorporation. A public company cannot commence its business until it is granted a "Certificate of Commencement of business".

Special privileges of a Private Company

Unlike a private a public company is subject to a number of regulations and restrictions as per the requirements of Companies Act, 1956. It is done to safeguard the interests of investors/shareholders of the public company. These privileges can be studied as follows :

a) Special privileges of all companies. The following privileges are available to every private company, including a private company which is subsidiary of a public company or deemed to be a public company :

1. A private company may be formed with only two persons as member. [Sec.12(1)]

2. It may commence allotment of shares even before the minimum subscription is subscribed for or paid (Sec. 69).

3. It is not required to either issue a prospectus to the public of file statement in lieu of a prospectus. (Sec 70 (3)]

4. Restrictions imposed on public companies regarding further issue of capital do not apply on private companies. [Sec 81 (3)]

5. Provisions of Sections 114 and 115 relating to share warrants shall not apply to it. (Sec. 14)

6. It need not keep an index of members. (Sec. 115)

7. It can commence its business after obtaining a certificate of incorporation. A certificate of commencement of business is not required. [Sec. 149 (7)]

8. It need not hold statutory meeting or file a statutory report [Sec. 165 (10)]

9. Unless the articles provide for a larger number, only two persons personally present shall form the quorum in case of a private company, while at least five member personally present form the quorum in case of a public company (Sec. 174).

10. A director is not required to file consent to act as such with the Registrar. Similarly, the provisions of the Act regarding undertaking to take up qualification shares and pay for them are not applicable to directors of a private companies [Sec. 266 (5) (b)]

11. Provisions in Section 284 regarding removal of directors by the company in general meeting shall not apply to a life director appointed by a private company on or before 1st April 1952 [Sec. 284 (1)]

13. In case of a private company, poll can be demanded by one member if not more than seven members are present, and by two member if not more than seven member are present. In case of a public company, poll can be demanded by persons having not less than one-tenth of the total voting power in respect of the resolution or holding shares on which an aggregate sum of not less than fifty thousand rupees has been paid-up (Sec. 179).

14. It need not have more than two directors, while a public company must have at least three directors (Sec. 252)

b) Privileges available to an independent private company (i.e. one which is not a subsidiary of a public company)

An independent private company is one which is not a subsidiary of a public company. The following special privileges and exemptions are available to an independent private company.

1. It may give financial assistance for purchase of or subscription for shares in the company itself.

2. It need not, like a public company, offer rights shares to the equity shareholders of the company.

3. The provisions of Sec. 85 to 90 as to kinds of share capital, new issues of share capital, voting, issue of shares with disproportionate rights, and termination of disproportionately excessive rights, do not apply to an independent private company.

4. A transfer or transferee of shares in an independent private company has no right of appeal to the Central Government against refusal by the company to register a transfer of its shares.

5. Sections 171 to 186 relating to general meeting are not applicable to an independent private company if it makes its own provisions by the Articles. Some provisions of these Sections are, however made expressly applicable.

6. Many provisions relating to directors of a public company are not applicable to an independent private company, e.g.

a) it need not have more than 2 directors.

b) The provisions relating to the appointment, retirement, reappointment, etc. of directors who are to retire by rotation and the procedure relating, there to are not applicable to it.

c) The provisions requiring the giving of 14 days' notice by new candidates seeking election as directors, as also provisions requiring the Central Government's sanction for increasing the number of directors by amending the Articles or otherwise beyond the maximum fixed in the Articles, are not applicable to it.

d) The provisions relating to the manner of filing up casual vacancies among directors and the duration of the period of office of directors and the requirements that the appointment of directors should be voted on individually and that the consent of each candidate for directorship should be filed with the Registrar, do not apply to it.

e) The provisions requiring the holding of a share qualification by directors and fixing the time within which such qualification is to be acquired and filing with the Registrar of a declaration of share qualification by each director are also not applicable to it.

f) It may, by its Articles, Provide special disqualifications for appointment of directors.

g) It may provide special grounds for vacation of office of a director.

    i) Sec. 295 prohibiting loans to directors does not apply to it. An interested director may participate or vote in Board's proceedings relating to his concern of interest in any contract of arrangement.

7. The restrictions as to the number of companies of which a person may be appointed managing director and the prohibition of such appointment for more than 5 years at a time, do not apply to it

8. The provisions prohibiting the subscribing for, or purchasing of, shares or debentures of other companies in the same group do not apply to it.

9. The provisions of Section 409 conferring power on the Central Government to present change in the Board of directors of a company where in the opinion of the

Central Government such change will be prejudicial to the interest of the company, do not apply to it.

When a Private company becomes a Public company

A private company shall become a public company in following cases :

i) By default : When it fails to comply with the essential requirements of a private company provided under Section 3 (1) (iii) Default in complying with the said three provisions shall disentitle a private company to enjoy certain privileges (Sec. 43).

ii) A private company which is a subsidiary of another public company shall be deemed to be a public company.

iii) By provisions of law - Section 43-A.

Section 43-A

a) Where not less than 25% of the paid-up share capital of a private company is held by one or more bodies" corporate such a private company shall become a public company from the data in which such 25% is held by body corporate [Sec. 43-A (1)]

b) Where the average annual turnover of a private company is not less than Rs. 10 crores during the relevant period, such a private company shall become a public company after the expiry of the period of three months from the last day of the relevant period when the accounts show the said average annual turnover [Sec. 43 A (1 A)].

c) When a private company holds not less than 25% of the paid up share capital of a public company the private company shall become a public company from the date on which the private company holds such 25% [Sec. 43A (IB)].

d) Where a private company accepts, after an invitation is made by an advertisement of receiving deposits from the public other than its members, directors or their relatives, such private company shall become a public company [Sec. 43A (IC)].

iv) **By Conversion :** When the private company converts itself into a public company by altering its Articles in such a manner that they no longer include essential requirements of a private company under Section 3 (1) (iii). On the data of such alternations, it shall cease to be private company. It shall comply with the procedure of converting itself into a public company [Sec. 44].

The Articles of Association of such a public company may continue to have the three restrictions and may continue to have two directors and less than seven members.

Within 3 months of such a conversion. Registrar of Companies shall be intimated. The Registrar shall delete the word 'Private' before the words 'Limited' in the name of the company and shall also make necessary alternations in the certificate of incorporation.

III. On the basis of Control

On the basis of control, a company may be classified into :

1. Holding companies, and

2. Subsidiary Company

1. Holding Company [Sec. 4(4)]. A company is known as the holding company of another company if it has control over the other company. According to Sec 4(4) a company is deemed to be the holding company of another if, but only if that other is its subsidiary.

A company may become a holding company of another company in either of the following three ways :-

a) by holding more than fifty per cent of the normal value of issued equity capital of the company; or

b) By holding more than fifty per cent of its voting rights;

or

c) by securing to itself the right to appoint, the majority of the directors of the other company , directly or indirectly.

The other company in such a case is known as a "Subsidiary company". Though the two companies remain separate legal entities, yet the affairs of both the companies are managed and controlled by the holding company. A holding company may have any number of subsidiaries. The annual accounts of the holding company are required to disclose full information about the subsidiaries.

2. Subsidiary Company. [Sec. 4 (I)]. A company is know as a subsidiary of another company when its control is exercised by the latter (called holding company) over the former called a subsidiary company. Where a company (company S) is subsidiary of another company (say Company H), the former (Company S) becomes the subsidiary of the controlling company (company H).

IV. On the basis of Ownership of companies

a) **Government Companies.** A Company of which not less than 51% of the paid up capital is held by the Central Government of by State Government or Government singly or jointly is known as a Government Company. It includes a company subsidiary to a government company. The share capital of a government company may be wholly or partly owned by the government, but it would not make it the agent of the government . The auditors of the government company are appointed by the government on the advice of the Comptroller and Auditor General of India. The Annual Report along with the auditor's report are placed before both the House of the parliament. Some of the examples of government companies are - Mahanagar Telephone Corporation Ltd., National Thermal Power Corporation Ltd., State Trading Corporation Ltd. Hydroelectric Power Corporation Ltd. Bharat Heavy Electricals Ltd. Hindustan Machine Tools Ltd. etc.

b) **Non-Government Companies.** All other companies, except the Government Companies, are called non-government companies. They do not satisfy the characteristics of a government company as given above.

V. On the basis of Nationality of the Company

a) **Indian Companies :** These companies are registered in India under the Companies Act. 1956 and have their registered office in India. Nationality of the members in their case is immaterial.

b) **Foreign Companies :** It means any company incorporated outside India which has an established place of business in India [Sec. 591 (I)]. A company has an established place of business in India if it has a specified place at which it carries on business such as an office, store house or other premises with some visible indication premises. Section 592 to 602 of Companies Act, 1956 contain provisions applicable to foreign companies functioning in India.

2.6 SUMMARY

Company may be defined as group of persons associated together to achieve some common objective. A company formed and registered under the Companies Act has certain special features, which reveal the nature of a company. These characteristics are also called the advantages of a company because as compared with other business organizations, these are in fact, beneficial for a company. Companies can be classified into five categories according to the mode of incorporation on the basis of number of members, on the basis of control, on the basis of ownership and on the basis of nationality of the company.

2.8 KEYWORDS

Company: A company means a body of individuals associated

together for a common objective, which may be business for profit or for some charitable purposes.

Registered Company: A registered company is one which is formed and registered under the Indian Companies Act, 1956 or

under any earlier Companies Act in force in India.

Public Company: A public company means a company which

is not a private company. Any seven or more persons can

join

hands to form a public company.

Holding Company: A company shall be deemed to be the holding company to another if that other is its subsidiary.

Unlimited Company: A company not having any limit on the liability of its member is called an unlimited company.

2.8 SELF ASSESSMENT QUESTIONS

1. Define 'Company'. What are its essential characteristics ?

2. Explain the special privileges of a private company as compared to a public company.

3. Bring out the difference between partnership and company form of organization.

4. Write notes on :

   a) Chartered Companies

   b) Government Companies

5. Classify company form of organization on the basis of liability of members.

2.9 SUGGESTED READINGS

P.P.S. Gogna, Mercantile Law, S.Chand & Company, New

Delhi. N.D. Kapoor, Company Law, Sultan Chand & Sons, New Delhi. S.C. Aggarwal, Company Law, Dhanpat Rai Publications, New Delhi.

S.K. Aggarwal, Business Law, Galgotia Publishing Company, New Delhi. G.K. Varshney, Elements of Business Law, S Chand & Co., New Delhi